Road to DESTINY

Margaret A. Sowemimo

Updated Edition 2014

Copyright © 2004, 2014

Margaret Adeola Sowemimo

All rights reserved. No part of this book may be reproduced in any form, except for the inclusion of brief quotations in a review, without the prior permission of the author in writing.

Unless otherwise noted, all scripture is taken from the New King James Version. Copyright © 1982 by Thomas Nelson, Inc. Used by permission. All rights reserved.

To order additional copies of this contact us:
Margaret Sowemimo
P.O. Box 800
Powder Springs, GA 30127
678-949-8883 or
www.chosenremnant.org
www.harvestlandicc.org
Email: chosenremnant@gmail.com

Amazon.com

Printed in the USA

ISBN # 978-0-9752974-0-7

TABLE OF CONTENTS

ACKNOWLEDGEMENTS .... *i*

PREFACE .... *iii*

Chapter 1: **D**ream 1
Chapter 2: **E**xpectation 7
Chapter 3: **S**etback 13
Chapter 4: **T**esting 19
Chapter 5: **I**ntervention 29
Chapter 6: **N**urturing 39
Chapter 7: **Y**ieldedness 45

Chapter 8: Conclusion..55

Learning from My Mistakes 59

Testimonies 62

ACKNOWLEDGEMENTS

I want to express my appreciation to my parents for their sacrifice which got me to where I am today. I want to especially acknowledge my late father, Albert Oladipo Soetan, for showing me what a loving father looks like. He contributed immensely to the relationship I now have with my Heavenly Father.

To my siblings and friends from different parts of the world, who have been my cheerleaders as I navigate the road to destiny, thank you so much. I want to thank my sister Ann Edu for her support and also making sure I stay focused.

Special mention goes to these friends for their continued support through prayer and words of encouragement; Patience Enenmoh, Ike Okoli, Helen Delaney, Melanie Johnson, Tonya Cobb, Vanessa Cook and Oladipo Obisesan.

Williams Uma, thank you for allowing God to use you to bring me to Him. That step of obedience is why I am where I am today in my relationship with the Lord as I continue to follow the path chosen for me by Him.

I want to thank my husband for his encouragement and selfless effort to see that I get this book revised. Our three children, Cecilia, Frederick, and Joshua, thank you for being there for me.

To my Heavenly Father, thank you so much for being the GREATEST DAD. What a blessing to be able to be myself with you through the fun times and the serious times we have together.

To you, Holy Spirit, thank you for being a loving Teacher. Even in the times I was slow in responding to your prompting, you gently reminded me again. There were times I just could not connect the dots; thanks for bringing clarity to me in those moments.

What can I say about the Lover of my soul? I love you so much and would not be writing this if you had not taken the first step to love me when I was still in sin. The desire of my heart is to love you more. Lord Jesus, thank you for being my Master, my Savior, and my Friend.

PREFACE

God knew you before you were conceived in your mother's womb. He had a plan in mind for your life; you are not here by chance, but rather because you are destined for great things in God. However, unless you let Him lead, you cannot fulfill His real purpose for your life. God does not define or look at greatness the way we do.

John the Baptist was a great man who walked the earth. He was great because he fulfilled God's purpose for his life. He came as a forerunner for Jesus Christ, and he was just that. John lived in the desert and ate locusts and wild honey. There is no record that John amassed wealth for himself while on earth. His focus was on fulfilling what God sent him here to do.

You may say, "I am already successful and have need of nothing." This is wonderful, but if God had called you to be a pastor, and you are a successful CEO of a corporation, totally focused on the market place, with no time to do God's will, your success means nothing, because you are in the wrong place doing the wrong thing. The same applies to you if you are called to the market place to minister, and you choose the pulpit—it will be wasted time. It is sometimes easier to go for the familiar, because doing God's will is challenging; but He will not leave you alone.

This book will assist you in understanding what you may encounter on the road to fulfilling your destiny. It will encourage you not to give up, but to continue in the direction that God has mapped out for you as you progress on the road towards your destiny.

The book can be used as a personal devotional, or for a group study. When used for a group study, it will help foster communication and exchange of thoughts on the challenges each person is facing. You will be encouraged when you hear what others are going through and how God is strengthening them in the midst of their challenges.

As a mature Christian, you could do the study with the young Christians whom you are mentoring. It will help them realize early the challenges one faces as you work out the plan and purpose of God for your life. Allow them to do more of the talking during the discussion; this will enable you to hear their heart.

Please understand there is no stupid question. Therefore, be free and transparent in sharing your heart as you do this study. You must understand that you cannot fulfill the plan of God because you are astute: You fulfill it because God is leading and guiding you by His Spirit.

What is DESTINY? It is the will of God, the conclusion or the destination of a thing.

The Lord formed your inward parts, meaning he purchased you before you were born, while you were still in the womb. This makes it clear that salvation is for all. After we are born, we decide to either serve God or self.

He covered you in your mother's womb; this means he wove you for a future purpose. God skillfully wrought you, meaning he shaped or fashioned you. Because He is the one who created you, He knows what you are best suited for in life.

¹²Indeed, the darkness shall not hide from You, But the night shines as the day; The darkness and the light are both alike to You. ¹³ For You formed my inward parts; You covered me in my mother's womb. ¹⁴I will praise You, for I am fearfully and wonderfully made; Marvelous are Your works, And that my soul knows very well. ¹⁵My frame was not hidden from You, When I was made in secret, And skillfully wrought in the lowest parts of the earth. ¹⁶Your eyes saw my substance, being yet unformed. And in Your book they all were written, The days fashioned for me, When as yet there were none of them. ¹⁷How precious also are Your thoughts to me, O God! How great is the sum of them! ¹⁸If I should count them, they would be more in number than the sand; When I awake, I am still with You. (Psalm 139:12-18)

God created you for a specific purpose; you need to believe that. In Ezekiel 37 the Lord asked Ezekiel in the valley of dry bones if the bones can live; Ezekiel answered, "God, only you know." When the Lord reveals his plan to us, it sometimes seems impossible to accomplish. This is good because we then learn to lean on Him.

God used the valley of dry bones to show Ezekiel that with Him nothing is impossible. The bones may be lifeless now, but by His Word and Breath life will be restored. Maybe for you too things are looking dead at the moment; the Giver of life can restore things to their original positions or better. Let us explore together what we encounter as we take this exciting journey with Him towards our destiny.

I believe you have a divine purpose, but unless you submit your will to the Lord, you cannot fulfill the divine purpose. A rich man who uses his money to help people but chooses not to serve God is doing a good thing, but his destination after death without a relationship with Christ will be hell.

> *[6]But we are all like an unclean thing, And all our righteousnesses are like filthy rags; We all fade as a leaf, And our iniquities, like the wind, Have taken us away. (Isaiah 64:6)*

We cannot earn eternal life; Jesus paid the price with His blood. He is the Way to God. There is no other way. When you allow him to take over your life, you will walk in the fullness of His plan for you. The plan of God for your life is much bigger than any plan you could have for yourself.

> *[17]How precious also are Your thoughts to me, O God! How great is the sum of them! [18]If I should count them, they would be more in number than the sand; When I awake, I am still with you. (Psalm 139:17-18)*

When I was in my teens, I had a dream...

I saw two ladies, who were best friends, (I will call them "A" and "B" for clarity). A was preparing for her wedding; I saw her with her fiancée. Next to them, I saw an already dug grave, even though they could not see it. I perceived B was not happy about the wedding because she wanted the man for herself. She devised a plan to get A killed so she could marry her fiancée.

I stood there watching, though no one could see me. Before I knew it, A and her fiancée started arguing and just as quickly as it started they were both dead (you have to pardon me, because I am just relating what I saw; you may say what caused the argument? I do not know, but I knew that B was responsible). I immediately made up my mind to go to heaven to talk to God on their behalf. I started my journey, the next minute I found myself in front of this beautiful gate; the only way to open the gate is through worship.

The gate had on it all kinds of beautiful stones, very big gems and heavy gates. As I continued to worship, it felt like others joined me in worship. The experience was so beautiful that words cannot fully describe it.

While worshiping, the gates opened, and I went in. I found myself in what looked like a conference room. I saw twelve men sitting at the table; One of them got up to ask me what I wanted; I told him I wanted to talk to God, but he said I could not talk with Him. I went on to say I would not leave until I talked to Him. He then asked me what the problem was; I related my story thus:

A was planning to marry this guy (as I started to relate the story they all appeared before everyone; I could point to each person as I relayed my message). Because B was jealous, she got them killed. I said I believed she was the one who deserved to die rather than the couple. I went on to say; "I will not leave unless I'm allowed to take A and her fiancée back with me. It's OK for you to keep B."

The man who had asked me the question said I should wait for him to check whether God would allow them to go with me. He went in, then came back and said God told him I could take A and her fiancée back, but B had to stay. I left and immediately found myself on a road. The next thing I knew I was back on earth. Between leaving and arriving on earth was about a minute.

At the time, it made no sense to me; I was very young, but the dream stayed with me. However, since I could not understand it, I did nothing about the dream, but it stayed in the back of my mind. I shared it with my dad, but he was just happy I came back. He never made any comment on the dream.

The Lord speaks again on the dream:

In 1995, I was at a retreat in St. Paul, Minnesota. After the activities of the day, on my way back to the room, the Holy Spirit spoke to me: "Remember the dream you had as a young child?" and I said, "Yes." He said, "God has called you to be one that will stand in the gap for the oppressed." He continued, "This is what you did for the couple: You stood in the gap; you went to the Father on their behalf, and life was restored to them."

I have discovered that God uses me in deliverance, in standing in the gap to fight spiritual oppression. In addition, I could perceive their intentions without been told. This is another area of gifting that the Lord has endowed me with.

I was about fourteen when I had the dream; it was close to twenty-two years later when I understood the full meaning of the dream. Note that I was not saved at the time, but God nevertheless had an assignment for me. He was already unfolding it, waiting for me to surrender to His will. I could have made other choices in life that would have led me through a different road. I could have been very successful, too, but would have missed the real reason I was created. I thank God; the path He carved out for me is gradually unfolding before me.

The first step on the journey is to have a personal relationship with the Lord Jesus Christ. As a young child, I did have a desire to serve the Lord, and I served the best way I knew. It did not mean I had a relationship with the Lord, but God knew I was seeking, and from time to time I would experience Him in a special way. Those experiences did not make me commit my life completely to Him. He has given me many dreams after that dream; He knows where He wants to take me, and committing my life to Him began the process of walking in my divine destiny.

The Lord began directing my path, and, although I messed up sometimes, He gently redirected me. I have begun the journey that will continue until eternity. I thank God; He leads and I just follow. I hope you enjoy reading <u>The Road to Destiny</u>, and I pray it will be a blessing to you as well as help you in understanding why sometimes things are not as smooth as you want them to be as you try to walk in God's divine destiny for your life.

Chapter 1
DREAM

direction, destination, divine purpose

A glimpse into the future… God gives you the privilege of having a sneak preview of His plan for your life.

Whatever the Lord shows you is either part of His plan for your life or the ultimate place He wants to take you. The plan for your life, as far as God is concerned, is settled. What remains is for you is to walk in it until you reach the destination.

The easiest way to get there is to rely on the direction of Holy Spirit. If you try to make it happen yourself, it will eventually take you longer to get there, or the accomplishment of His purpose may never come to fruition.

Since He has the blueprint, He knows each step you need to take to get there. You have to trust Him.

In Genesis 37:5-10, we see that God gave Joseph two dreams relating to His future.

> *[5]Now Joseph had a dream, and he told it to his brothers; and they hated him even more. [6]So he said to them, "Please hear this dream which I have dreamed: [7]"There we were, binding sheaves in the field. Then behold, my sheaf arose and also stood upright; and indeed your sheaves stood all around and bowed down to my sheaf." [8]And his brothers said to him,*

"Shall you indeed reign over us? Or shall you indeed have dominion over us?" So they hated him even more for his dreams and for his words. ⁹Then he dreamed still another dream and told it to his brothers, and said, "Look, I have dreamed another dream. And this time, the sun, the moon, and the eleven stars bowed down to me." ¹⁰So he told it to his father and his brothers; and his father rebuked him and said to him, "What is this dream that you have dreamed? Shall your mother and I and your brothers indeed come to bow down to the earth before you?"

Joseph's family understood what the dream meant, and it immediately brought envy and jealousy. Even Joseph did not know this road would be a very challenging road. Joseph was only seventeen when the Lord revealed His plan for his life. You start off with where you are going, but start to walk towards the goal.

About fifteen years ago, I had a dream; I went to do ministry in a country where the people looked like me but did not talk like me. At the said time, our pastor was from Jamaica. My brain figured out it must be Jamaica, but this dream played out over a decade later. I had the opportunity to go to Kenya and Uganda to do some leadership training. We used an interpreter; even though some spoke English, the majority did not. They did look like me—but they did not speak like me.

At the time of the dream, I had no connection with these two countries. This is why it is important not to worry about how we will be called to follow God; we just have to trust Him. If you think you have it figured out, God will probably come in a different way.

Here is one more dream that will encourage you. I was twenty-eight years old at the time:

In the dream, I was walking down a path, and a military officer was with some people. He came to me and introduced himself as Sam Doe [real name withheld]. When I woke up, I remembered the name vividly because it was such a unique name which I had not heard before. I asked my brother, who worked for the ministry of information about it, and he told me that was the name of the Minister of Internal Affairs. He asked me why I wanted to know, and I said, "Because I met him in my dream."

You should have seen the look on my brother's face; he did not say anything, but I knew he did not see how it could happen. A year later, I started working for a company involved in business services. One of the directors was in the City Capital and wanted to introduce me to some people in the company registration office who are pivotal for our business.

The next morning, my boss picked me up to go with him to have breakfast at his friends'. When we got there, we were ushered into the dining room. A man came in, stretched out his hand to me and introduced himself as Sam Doe (remember the real name is being withheld—but it was the same name as that of the man in the dream).

I stood there in amazement. I finally said I dreamt a year ago that we met—and here we are. Wow! God is good! When I had the dream, I was not even connected to the one who would help to fulfill the dream, just as Joseph at the time of his dream was not connected to the one who would help to fulfill the dream.

Yours may not be a dream, but a vision or prophetic word that points you towards your destiny. In 1998, I was given a word: I should go to my country to minister in front of a large group of people. At the time, I had no intention of going back and did not have many connections with the people except for my family that still lived there. Ten years later, I found myself ministering in my country in front of thousands of people. I will not go into the details of how it happened (if you want to know, email me, and I will tell you). All you need to take from this is the fact that God is faithful. Trust Him for what He has spoken concerning your life, and you will see all come to pass in Jesus' name.

If I want to sew a dress, I look at the pattern (usually the finished outfit is shown on the package), before cutting the material for the sewing. I have to use different pieces of the pattern to complete the outfit. The same way the Lord continues to put together the pieces for your life until you become who He wants you to be.

FOOD FOR THOUGHT

I am sure that for Joseph his were good dreams. The problem was that Joseph was not the first-born—so how would he end up ruling over his brothers?

Whenever you have a dream, vision, or prophetic word from the Lord, you cannot visualize how it will be fulfilled. This is because everything in the natural world reveals you are either not in a position to bring it to pass, or you just do not qualify for what God wants to do in your life. Even when you know you do not qualify; but you can rejoice in the fact that He qualifies you.

EXERCISE

1. Write down the word, vision, or dream the Lord has given you concerning ministry or His purpose for your life._____
   _____
   _____
   _____

2. Even if you are not sure of what He said or have not heard anything, write that down._____
   _____
   _____
   _____

3. In what area of ministry do you have the desire to be used by the Lord, and why?_____
   _____
   _____
   _____

4. Share a dream you had and how the Lord fulfilled it._____
   _____
   _____
   _____

Prayer Point:

God, who gave the dream, vision, or word is the one who will fulfill it. If it is yet to be, thank Him now for it. You may not know how it will be fulfilled, but, by thanking Him, you are letting Him know you have faith that it will be fulfilled

MORE NOTES FROM GROUP SHARING

Chapter 2
EXPECTATION

hope, anticipation

While you are expecting great things, the enemy starts to plot to thwart God's plan and purpose for your life.

I did not fully understand the dream, but deep within me the dream stayed, and I knew God had a call on my life. I still could not figure out how I could go to heaven to talk to God, but years later the Lord gave me the explanation of the dream.

> *[24]God is a spirit, and they that worship him must worship him in spirit and in truth. (John 4:24)*

The enemy has come against me numerous times to try to destroy me, but the Lord has always protected me, because of the seed He put in me that must bear fruit.

The original intent of the brothers was to kill Joseph, but Reuben and Judah were used by God without their knowing, to prevent the shedding of Joseph's blood.

All of Joseph's siblings except for Benjamin were from different mothers. Joseph was very naïve because the dream involved the whole family, and he should not have said it openly like he did. He probably was too excited to know he would rule over them.

Sometimes we have to be careful with whom we share the things of God concerning our lives. However, in Joseph's case, it helped to bring about the fulfillment of God promise to get Joseph to Egypt. What the enemy meant for evil, the Lord turned around for good.

Joseph's expectation was to become a ruler over his siblings. A lot of different things must have run through his mind after the dream, but I believe none of them lined up with the way God was going to unfold it.

David was anointed King over Israel at a young age, but he did not ascend the throne until he was thirty years of age. David had to run for his life because Saul was out to kill him, and he suffered rejection and humiliation. But, in the end, He became king over Israel. I am sure that, like Joseph. he must have had high expectations but never bargained for the challenges that followed.

Our Father is the master planner, and, even when we do not have a way, He does. Remember: He started this whole process and He is omniscient (all-knowing). Is there anything that is ever going to take place that He does not already know? If you can think of any example, share with your group now.

God had already set a course of action in motion for Joseph. For example, why did the traders come at the time they did? It was all part of God's divine plan. Joseph's brothers thought they were getting rid of Joseph. However, God was using them to bring about the fulfillment of the dream He had told Abraham that his descendants would be strangers in a foreign land for four hundred years but would later come out with many possessions.

> *¹³Then He said to Abram: "Know certainly that your descendants will be strangers in a land that is not theirs, and will serve them, and they will afflict them four hundred years. ¹⁴And also the nation whom they serve I will judge; afterward they shall come out with great possessions." (Genesis 15:13)*

I have seen many people who were very excited about what the Lord was going to do in their lives, but the excitement was short lived because things fell apart and everything went in the opposite direction.

You must understand that many times things will go in the opposite direction to what God promised before you see the fulfillment of the dream. Joseph hit the bottom first (the pit) before getting to the top.

When I finished college, I had high expectations of becoming a career woman. I was going to make a name for myself in the corporate world. I always found favor wherever I went. After I earned my master's degree in the U.S., I went back to my country with the hope of getting a well-paying job. My father had the connections, but, in my situation, every connection failed. Others who used the same people had no issue getting a job. I could not figure out what was going on in my situation.

In 1986 I took a vacation to England with my sister. We had heard of a woman who was very strong prophetically, and we both decided to go see her. She said many things of which the majority had come to pass in both my life and my sister's today.

I left the place disappointed because she said I had two roads I could take and each would lead to success for me, but she believed the best road for me is the one that would be a voluntary job. She saw a strong call in me and gave me some scriptures to read for clarity but strongly advised I take the ministry part. That is not what I was expecting; I was hoping she would see me get a job.

I eventually found a job. I worked there for a little while before traveling back to the U.S. I came to join my husband because he also could not find a job. I look back now and I am thankful I chose the path I did, because no amount of money can compensate for my relationship with the Lord plus the joy of being used by Him.

You may feel like your hope or expectation has been dashed. Trust me: God is working, and in the best way, to thrust you into the center of His will for you. It will all make sense in the end. Be encouraged by this verse.

> [11]*For I know the plans I have for you," says the* LORD. *"They are plans for good and not for disaster, to give you a future and a hope." (Jeremiah 29:11 NLT)*

EXERCISE

1. What expectation did you have after the Lord gave you a word, dream, or vision? _____
   _____
   _____
   _____

2. With the expectation you have, do you think it will be difficult to fulfill it, or do you already have an idea of how it will play out? _____
   _____
   _____
   _____

3. Are you excited to see it happen, or do you not really care? _
   _____
   _____
   _____

4. Do you believe in the faithfulness of God to bring it to pass?
   _____
   _____
   _____
   _____

Meditate on this verse, discuss it as a group, and use it as a prayer point. Thank The Lord also for the things you are expecting Him to do in your life.

*⁵ My soul, wait silently for God alone,
For my expectation is from Him. (Psalm 62:5)*

MORE NOTES FROM GROUP SHARING

_____
_____
_____
_____
_____
_____
_____
_____
_____
_____
_____
_____
_____
_____
_____
_____
_____
_____
_____
_____
_____
_____
_____
_____
_____

Chapter 3
SETBACK

unexpected delay and disappointment

It is something you did not anticipate. You are expecting the journey to be smooth, but now you hit bumps on the way. Things are not going as you envisaged they would.

Joseph must have been disappointed, but, at the fullness of time, things became clear to him. The brothers would later come to the realization of what they meant for evil in the life of Joseph, but God used them for the good of all of them in the end. People will celebrate you and the goodness of God in your life. Remain focused and committed to Him.

> *[21] But Reuben heard it, and he delivered him out of their hands, and said, "Let us not kill him." [22] And Reuben said to them, "Shed no blood, but cast him into this pit which is in the wilderness, and do not lay a hand on him" -- that he might deliver him out of their hands, and bring him back to his father. [23] So it came to pass, when Joseph had come to his brothers, that they stripped Joseph of his tunic, the tunic of many colors that was on him. [24] Then they took him and cast him into a pit. And the pit was empty; there was no water in it. [25] And they sat down to eat a meal. Then they lifted their eyes and looked, and there was a company of Ishmaelites, coming from Gilead with their camels, bearing spices, balm, and myrrh, on their way to carry them down to Egypt. [26] So Judah said to his brothers, "What profit is*

there if we kill our brother and conceal his blood? ²⁷"Come and let us sell him to the Ishmaelites, and let not our hand be upon him, for he is our brother and our flesh." And his brothers listened. ²⁸Then Midianite traders passed by; so the brothers pulled Joseph up and lifted him out of the pit, and sold him to the Ishmaelites for twenty shekels of silver. And they took Joseph to Egypt. (Genesis 37:21-28)

FOOD FOR THOUGHT:

Looking at the situation of Joseph, it seemed like a delay or setback; but, if Joseph's brothers had not planned to kill him, Reuben would not have suggested throwing him into the pit. Reuben wanted to come back to rescue him. God was not going to allow Reuben to do that; hence, the Ishmaelite traders soon came along. Judah suggested he should be sold instead of killing him. God was working in all of these things, using the brothers as the instrument without their knowledge.

The good news is this: If you are truly serving the Lord, the devil may try to kill you, but he cannot succeed. What looks like a setback will be your step forward. God will use people in your life to channel what God wants to do. You may see them as enemies, but they are needed on your road to destiny.

Those you thought were your enemies were actually instruments in the hand of the Lord. I do not believe that a Christian can grow and mature without any setback, because the challenges strengthen us.

The devil tried to kill Jesus as a child through Herod's edict that all male children two years and below should be killed. But Jesus escaped. Shortly after the birth of Moses, the devil used Pharaoh to order the midwives to kill all Hebrew male children at birth. However, God intervened and used the same people who had orders to kill the Hebrew boys to be the ones to spare them. **WHAT A MIGHTY GOD WE SERVE!**

> [1]*The king's heart is in the hand of the* LORD,
> *Like the rivers of water; He turns it wherever He*
> *wishes. (Proverbs 21:1)*

God can influence the heart of anyone He wants, to accomplish His purpose. Stay encouraged, knowing He will do what is needed to enable you to obtain favor.

After I got saved, I attended a holiness church where we were grounded in the Word of God. However, we were not allowed to use our gifts even though we were taught about the gifts of the Spirit. One day, I prophesied; the pastor came to the pulpit to announce the church did not believe in prophecy. It was after the announcement I realized I really could not use my God-given gift in that church.

Even though, like others, I was not given the opportunity to use my gift, the Lord continued to teach me many things in my prayer time.

With each Sunday that passed, I quickly realized God's purpose for my life could not be fulfilled in that environment, but stayed because the Lord had not asked us to leave. Even though I was a baby Christian at the time, I asked to be shown in the Bible the things that my spirit was not agreeing with, and majority of the times they were just man-made rules.

I was referred to as the one that troubled Israel. Let me cite an example of what we could not do: We were planning a friend's wedding, and I offered to bring fried rice but was told I could not because it would be sinful. I was shocked and asked that they show me in the Bible. I was told it is expensive and not everyone can afford it. I told them it was one of the cheapest things we could cook here in the U.S. After a while, dissatisfaction set in' we just waited for the Lord to release us, which He eventually did.

What I did not realize is that it was all part of His plan. He started me off at that church because I needed to grow in the Word, and they had a solid foundation in the Word. With the foundation I got there, I could find balance; I did not go to either extreme. Even though I had a very agonizing experience there, I knew later that I was exactly where I needed to be in the plan of God.

Like Joseph, I knew I could only find solace in the Lord, and every setback drew me closer to Him. I do not know what you are experiencing at the moment, but be encouraged, knowing God is in the midst of it. He is working on your behalf even though you do not see it. Your setback is just a temporary delay which is needed to set the stage for the next step. It is a step forward, and you will later see it that way. Try to enjoy the season.

EXERCISE

1. Write down the setback you experienced after the Lord revealed His purpose for your life._____
   _____
   _____
   _____
   _____

2. How did you keep yourself encouraged, and if you are still in that stage, what are you doing to stay encouraged? _____
   _____
   _____
   _____
   _____

3. What did you learn, or, if still in the situation, what *are* you learning? Share with the group._____
   _____
   _____
   _____
   _____

[28]And we know that all things work together for good to those who love God, to those who are the called according to His purpose. (Romans 8:28)

[5] Every word of God is pure; He is a shield to those who put their trust in Him. (Proverbs 30:5)

Meditate on those two scriptures and let them encourage you. Hopefully, you now understand your setbacks were things He was using to train you for the call. Give Him praise for them. If you are angry, tell Him how you feel.

MORE NOTES FROM GROUP SHARING

Chapter 4
TESTING

putting to the proof; a means of examining or evaluating something; a trial

Your testing period is the time to sit back and to reflect on what God promised and how the setback directly applies in your situation. Joseph was sold into slavery; this was very contrary to the dream the Lord gave him. A time of testing is the perfect time to figure out how much you trust God and His word. As Samuel said, the strength of Israel will never lie. Be encouraged by this scripture, Psalm 138:2 in the New Living Translation:

> *[2]I bow before your holy Temple as I worship. I praise your name for your unfailing love and faithfulness; for your promises are backed by all the honor of your name. (Psalm 138:2 NLT)*

Joseph might not have fully understood what was happening to him because of the challenges he faced—and he may have decided to let the dreams go. We can learn this one thing from Joseph: He remained faithful to God. He never displayed a bad attitude, even though he suffered betrayal and abandonment by his family.

He chose not to disobey God in the time of temptation. Potiphar's wife wanted to sleep with Joseph; he refused by running out of the room, leaving behind his garment. Potiphar's wife lied against him, which landed him in prison.

If Joseph had agreed to sleep with her, it may have made life "more enjoyable" for Joseph, because she would have favored him more. However, eventually there would have been repercussions.

What he was doing in darkness would come to light, even if he was never found out; he would be in that house "enjoying" life but every day living in fear of being caught. Joseph would have aborted the dream. The lack of compromise on his part sent him to prison. The prison was a step forward, even though he did not know it at the time. Joseph was a step closer to fulfilling his destiny. You must decide, no matter how challenging things get, not to compromise.

Compromising sometime seems a quick fix, but taking such a step may derail you from the path God originally mapped out for you. Some may never recover, while some are able to.

Testing time is no fun at all; you feel as if God has abandoned you. Sometimes you repent every day because you think you are going through your trials because you sinned—but that is not always the case. When David ran from Saul after being anointed as king over Israel, it was not because he did anything wrong. Saul was after his life to kill him, in the same way that Joseph's brothers tried to kill him. God was using the persecution in David's life to develop his character in preparation for the throne. It is only a broken vessel that can walk in humility and obedience before God.

My time of testing was when the persecution started for me in the church mentioned earlier. I was called 'the one that troubled Israel'. I did not at the time know that the pastor had discussed me with his inner circle.

I shared a dream with the pastor concerning what I believed God was showing me about the church. (I did not outright go to my pastor to share the dream. I checked first with our overseer, and he gave me the go ahead.)

After sharing the dream, the next week the pastor preached about people and their dreams and how they feel that God is talking through them. Sincerely, God bearing me witness, I never knew he was talking about me. I went about my business after the service bubbly as usual.

Come Thursday morning, the pastor called me early at work to let me know that the Wednesday message he preached was about me, in case I did not get it. He also accused me of attending the Women Aglow meeting, and taking people from the church to the meetings (our church was really against members' attending any other ministries for anything).

Here I was on the phone having never attended a Women Aglow meeting but being accused of taking people to the meeting. Moreover, I did not even realize the preaching was about me. The attacks did not cease. When the pastor found out the accusations were false, he did not apologize.

Eight years after I left the ministry, I got the opportunity to go to the Women Aglow meeting to minister. God sees what we go through for the Kingdom. This would be my first time going, and I refer to it as the fullness of time for me. I was persecuted and falsely accused by the pastor for going at a time I knew nothing about The Women Aglow.

I wanted to leave the ministry because I knew the pastor had made an enemy of me just because people frequently come to me asking for prayers. The pastor said I was trying to take over the church from him. God knows I did nothing out of the ordinary. I prayed for people just as others did. I kept a good attitude and continued to serve until the day the Lord released us to move on.

This was a great period of testing, because we had the choice of running off to some other church or staying where God wanted us regardless of the persecution. We chose to stay there. The sale of Joseph to the Midianites must have been the worst experience of his life. Joseph was a young man who did not know what fate awaited him in Egypt.

Even as a slave, Joseph found favor in the house of Potiphar. Joseph was not feeling sorry for himself but was diligent in his work and took very good care of Potiphar's household. It is recorded in Genesis 39 that God was with Joseph, and he prospered. Just because you are going through something difficult does not mean God is not with you. You may feel as if He has departed from you, but He promised never to leave you nor forsake you.

The challenges I faced did not stop me from thriving spiritually. The heaven over me opened because I focused more on using His gift in me to bless people outside of the church. I ministered to people at work and to friends outside of my church circle.

> [2]*The LORD was with Joseph, and he was a successful man; and he was in the house of his master the Egyptian.* [3]*And his master saw that the LORD was with him and that the LORD made all he did to prosper in his hand.* [4]*So Joseph found favor in his sight, and*

served him. Then he made him overseer of his house, and all that he had he put under his authority. ⁵So it was, from the time that he had made him overseer of his house and all that he had, that the LORD blessed the Egyptian's house for Joseph's sake; and the blessing of the LORD was on all that he had in the house and in the field. ⁶Thus he left all that he had in Joseph's hand, and he did not know what he had except for the bread which he ate. Now Joseph was handsome in form and appearance. (Genesis 39:2-6)

The Bible records that Joseph found favor in the house of Potiphar because God was with him. If God is with us, and we choose to display a bad attitude, we may hinder what He is trying to do. During the testing period, we must maintain a good attitude because it is our most vulnerable time. We can easily make the wrong decision, because we are trying to run away from the challenges rather than walk through them.

Joseph was favored of Potiphar, but Potiphar's wife lied against him because he refused to sleep with her (Genesis 39:7-23). Joseph was imprisoned because of this lie but, while in prison, he maintained a good attitude. Joseph found favor with the prison keeper and eventually he was put in command. His testing did not bring out the worst in him; instead, he continued to be diligent in his business.

²²And the keeper of the prison put Joseph in charge of all the prisoners who were in the prison. Whatever was done there, he was the one who did it. ²³The keeper of the prison paid no attention to anything that was in Joseph's charge, because the LORD was with him. And whatever he did, the LORD made it succeed. (Genesis 39:22-23)

Joseph eventually stood before Pharaoh. Do not run ahead of God stay where He has you until he moves you. It was really a painful experience for my family, especially me, but today I can truly say I am stronger and wiser.

*[29]Do you see a man who excels in his work?
He will stand before kings; He will not stand before unknown men. (*Proverbs 22:29*)*

Most of our friends abandoned us. We held on to the promise of God that He would never leave us nor forsake us. Jesus is a friend who sticks closer than a brother; the scripture came alive for my family in the season.

I thank God; He healed us from all the hurt, and I learned during my time of testing that my focus should be on Jesus. I did not decide to abandon God and fellowship with believers. Your testing time should draw you closer to God, not away from Him. He is your true source of strength. Quiet yourself so you can know what it is; you are meant to learn in the situation.

I learned submission to authority amidst the pain. I did not see how I could be a threat to the pastor. One of the sisters told the pastor I sent cards to the ladies in the church begging them to become my friend. I could not believe a Christian would cook up such a lie, nor that the pastor would believe without investigating. Some of the people have already reaped the fruit of what they did, but I am thankful that, in it all, everyone is back with God.

I have no hard feelings towards them. If they did not do what they did I would not have the intimate relationship I have with the Lord now. Furthermore, learning to stay in a situation I would rather walk away from was humbling, but God used it to teach me endurance. He knew there would be many more encounters for me in life. Even though I knew the person saw me as a threat, I still had to submit to God's appointed vessel for the season, He wanted me there.

Psalm 105 talks about how the word of the Lord tested Joseph, and how, in the end, the Word of the Lord came to pass. The challenges will pass, so do not lose faith; continue to look unto Jesus.

> [16]*Moreover He called for a famine in the land; He destroyed all the provision of bread.* [17]*He sent a man before them -- Joseph -- who was sold as a slave.* [18]*They hurt his feet with fetters, He was laid in irons.* [19]*Until the time that his word came to pass, The word of the LORD tested him.* [20]*The king sent and released him, The ruler of the people let him go free. (Psalm 105:16-20)*

The Joseph's testing brought the breakthrough to the Butler; the pain of Pharaoh, because of the dreams he could not interpret, brought the breakthrough to Joseph. Your pain sometimes will lead to the breakthrough of another. Paul and Silas' pain brought salvation to the jailer's household.

EXERCISE

1. Share with your friend a Bible character that walked in the call of God with no opposition. _____
   _____
   _____
   _____
   _____

2. Share the challenges you have faced and how you handled them. _____
   _____
   _____
   _____

3. What challenge(s) are you facing right now? _____
   _____
   _____
   _____
   _____
   _____

4. Share how you feel now, knowing the opposition or challenges you faced helped to mature you. _____
   _____
   _____
   _____
   _____
   _____

5. Write down the area of challenges in which you need prayer.
   _____
   _____
   _____
   _____

   MORE NOTES FROM GROUP SHARING
   _____
   _____
   _____
   _____
   _____
   _____
   _____
   _____
   _____
   _____
   _____
   _____
   _____
   _____
   _____
   _____
   _____
   _____
   _____
   _____

Chapter 5
INTERVENTION

interference, involvement

After a while, we had the sense that it was time to leave because our work was finished there. It became a struggle to leave now that we had the release from the Lord. We were involved with the children, and I had grown to love the kids. It is interesting that, when it all started, I wanted to leave, but, when the Lord finally gave the release, it was hard to.

We struggled with this for weeks. One day, I went to a drug store to get some stencils for my daughter for her class project. While I was trying to find the right aisle, a man approached me from behind without my knowing at first that he was there. He said, "You know when the Lord tells someone to move, it is always for something better." He talked about how he found it difficult to leave his well-established church for a church that was meeting at the hotel, because they did not have a building. He told me how he struggled with it but finally obeyed and left. He said that had been his best move.

I stood there in amazement, not saying anything to him; he just said everything we were struggling with at the time. I bought what I came to get and left. A few days later I had to get an outfit for my daughter at Marshall Departmental Store for another project at school. As I turned, I saw the man again; he said "Hello." I said, "Are you my angel, because you seem to be following me around?"

He told me to follow him because he wanted me to meet his wife; we looked everywhere but could not find the wife. She was on her knees behind me with a blue jacket almost as if she just showed up from nowhere. He introduced me as the lady he saw at the drug store a few days ago. She said, "If God says you should move, you need to move." She also said she wanted to reassure me that I would not remember the pain and the hurt, unless I chose to remember them, because God will bless me, and I will grow more spiritually.

I was too dumbfounded to speak, because the first time I did not say a word to the man, and here the wife is talking about the same thing. She went even further to comment on the hurt and pain. They must have been angels from God. I thanked her, walked away, and never saw them again.

Some weeks later, we decided to visit the home group of a Prophetic Ministry where I had taken a course on Praise and Worship. The lady who was to lead was not able to make it. She asked a man to do it. He said, "I really am not prepared for tonight," because he had been involved in some kind of accident and was on crutches. He said, "I asked the Lord what he wanted me to talk about, and the Lord said talk about the people who refuse to change. God is telling them to move, and they refuse to move" on and on he went. The rest is history; we got home that night, really prayed, and made up our mind to leave the church we were attending at the time.

This is how God intervened in our situation; the minute we said we were leaving we were persecuted the more. We knew we were engaged in warfare. We bathe ourselves in prayer continually. We were finally able to leave peacefully. Just as the lady I met in the departmental store said, it was true

freedom. For the first time, I was in an environment that allowed me to be me using the gift God graced me with to bless His people. The prophetic training and exposure we got here can be
referred to as the catalyst for the Ministries we now oversee.

God intervened in the life of Joseph by giving Pharaoh two dreams. It is such a beautiful and encouraging thing to know that God can use anyone and anything to fulfill His plan.

> *[14]Then Pharaoh sent and called Joseph, and they quickly brought him out of the pit. And when he had shaved himself and changed his clothes, he came in before Pharaoh. [15]And Pharaoh said to Joseph, "I have had a dream, and there is no one who can interpret it. I have heard it said of you that when you hear a dream you can interpret it." [16]Joseph answered Pharaoh, "It is not in me; God will give Pharaoh a favorable answer." [17]Then Pharaoh said to Joseph, "Behold, in my dream I was standing on the banks of the Nile. [18]Seven cows, plump and attractive, came up out of the Nile and fed in the reed grass. [19]Seven other cows came up after them, poor and very ugly and thin, such as I had never seen in all the land of Egypt. [20]And the thin, ugly cows ate up the first seven plump cows, [21]but when they had eaten them no one would have known that they had eaten them, for they were still as ugly as at the beginning. Then I awoke. [22]I also saw in my dream seven ears growing on one stalk, full and good. [23]Seven ears, withered, thin, and blighted by the east wind, sprouted after them, [24]and the thin ears swallowed up the seven good ears. And I told it to the magicians, but there was no one who could explain it to me." [25]Then Joseph said*

to Pharaoh, "The dreams of Pharaoh are one; God has revealed to Pharaoh what he is about to do. [26]The seven good cows are seven years, and the seven good ears are seven years; the dreams are one. [27]The seven lean and ugly cows that came up after them are seven years, and the seven empty ears blighted by the east wind are also seven years of famine. [28]It is as I told Pharaoh; God has shown to Pharaoh what he is about to do. [29]There will come seven years of great plenty throughout all the land of Egypt, [30]but after them there will arise seven years of famine, and all the plenty will be forgotten in the land of Egypt. The famine will consume the land, [31]and the plenty will be unknown in the land by reason of the famine that will follow, for it will be very severe. [32]And the doubling of Pharaoh's dream means that the thing is fixed by God, and God will shortly bring it about. [33]Now therefore let Pharaoh select a discerning and wise man, and set him over the land of Egypt. [34]Let Pharaoh proceed to appoint overseers over the land and take one-fifth of the produce of the land of Egypt during the seven plentiful years. [35]And let them gather all the food of these good years that are coming and store up grain under the authority of Pharaoh for food in the cities, and let them keep it. [36]That food shall be a reserve for the land against the seven years of famine that are to occur in the land of Egypt, so that the land may not perish through the famine." [37]This proposal pleased Pharaoh and all his servants. [38]And Pharaoh said to his servants, "Can we find a man like this, in whom is the Spirit of God?" [39]Then Pharaoh said to Joseph, "Since God has shown you all this, there is none so discerning and wise as you are. [40]You shall be over my house, and all my people shall order *themselves as you command. Only as regards the throne will I be greater than you." ⁴¹And Pharaoh said to Joseph, "See, I have set you over all the land of Egypt." ⁴²Then Pharaoh took his signet ring from his hand and put it on Joseph's hand, and clothed him in garments of fine linen and put a gold chain about his neck. ⁴³And he made him ride in his second chariot. And they called out before him, "Bow the knee!" Thus he set him over all the land of Egypt. ⁴⁴Moreover, Pharaoh said to Joseph, "I am Pharaoh, and without your consent no one shall lift up hand or foot in all the land of Egypt." ⁴⁵And Pharaoh called Joseph's name Zaphenath-paneah. And he gave him in marriage Asenath, the daughter of Potiphera priest of On. So Joseph went out over the land of Egypt. ⁴⁶Joseph was thirty years old when he entered the service of Pharaoh king of Egypt. And Joseph went out from the presence of Pharaoh and went through all the land of Egypt. (Genesis 41:14-46)*

No one in the land, except for Joseph, could interpret Pharaoh's dreams. The Baker and the Butler were part of the instruments that God used in the life of Joseph. If they had not come to the prison, there would have been no dreams to interpret for them. Even after the interpretation, Joseph told the Butler to remember him when he found favor in Pharaoh's eyes again. The Butler forgot all about Joseph for another two years.

It is very important to understand the lesson here: Promotion comes from God. He may use a man, as he used Pharaoh, but we cannot manipulate our way into getting His plan fulfilled. God makes all things beautiful in His own time. Joseph understood a lot about pain from being in Potiphar's house and in prison. He must have been very lonely, away from home and his family.

Sometimes, to see the fulfillment of God's plan, we may have to let some things go. It may be painful at first but will eventually be for the best. Sometimes God strips us of the familiar so our focus can be on Him. No family, no friends to help Joseph, but God remained His helper.

Even if the Butler remembered Joseph, I do not believe he could have just walked into Pharaoh's presence to share with him about Joseph. Pharaoh had his magicians who did his interpretations. Joseph was not needed two years prior.

Secondly, all the glory would not have gone to the Lord because it would have looked like the Butler got Joseph out of prison.

After we left the church, the people we thought were our friends either deserted us or stayed friends for a while. Looking back, now we can say that it was necessary, so we could shift our focus onto God instead of a man.

Joseph also had to leave his familiar surroundings, his family, and his father, especially to be able to focus on God. Some of these people did not need to be part of the next phase of our lives—nor that of Joseph. God started another chapter on our road to destiny. The things we were able to do, we could not have done at the Church, especially for me as a woman.

A good example of this is a lady who came to one of our meetings, and the Lord told me to take authority over the spirit of death. The Lord delivered her that night, but I still questioned—why death? She did not look like one to kill herself. Later, that night the friend who invited her to the meeting called to share with me that the lady had purposed to kill herself that weekend.

The lady heard of the conference on Friday and showed up Saturday. We found out later that she had suffered a lot of abuse from her husband, who was also a minister of the Gospel. Everyone saw her as the bad person, and she was just tired.

She loves the Lord and believes that God has a call on her life. The Lord delivered her; she went back to college to study something in the medical line.

The Lord knew that she had reached the end of her rope and could not take any more. He intervened in her situation. The same thing applies to our lives—the Lord will always intervene at the appropriate time. Be encouraged that He will not give you more than you can bear. He has not left you alone. He will come to your rescue. He promised not to give you more than you can bear.

> [13]*No temptation has overtaken you except such as is common to man; but God is faithful, who will not allow you to be tempted beyond what you are able, but with the temptation will also make the way of escape, that you may be able to bear it (1 Corinthians 10:13)*

What you are experiencing now someone has experienced before. If God delivered them and gave them hope, He will do the same for you. He made everything beautiful for us in His time, and He will do likewise for you.

The Lord did not intervene in the situation of the Hebrew boys (Shadrach, Meshach, and Abednego [Daniel 3:1-24]) before they went into the fire. He intervened *when* they got into the fire. When things get too hot for you on the road to destiny, the Lord will intervene. It is funny how we think we cannot go on and are ready to turn back, but He allows His grace to carry us when we feel we cannot endure any longer.

Be encouraged, if you have been calling out, and it seems like God is not hearing, His ear is not heavy that He cannot hear. He will show up at the right time!

EXERCISE

1. Share a challenging situation and how God intervened. _____
   _____
   _____
   _____
   _____

2. What did you learn from the situation? _____
   _____
   _____
   _____
   _____

3. Have you ever experienced any persecution? If yes, share your experience. _____
   _____
   _____
   _____
   _____

4. How did you handle it? _____
   _____
   _____
   _____
   _____

5. Looking back, how can you relate it to the purpose of God for your life?_____
_____
_____
_____

MORE NOTES FROM GROUP SHARING

Chapter 6
NURTURING

training, upbringing, supplying with nourishment

The hardship enhanced us. We came to realize God was doing something in us even though we preferred to leave the church, but we kept a good attitude. We came to a place of knowing we could not put our trust in anyone but God, because, just when we thought a person was going to come through for us, we received disappointment instead. We came to that realization that God was the one who gave us the vision and only God could bring it to pass.

The agonizing situation we went through turned us into nurturers, even as we were receiving nurturing too. We were able to talk about the hurt without the pain. We learned that God had to break our will and humble us, so we could face the next stage of our journey in total submission to Him.

God settled us into a new ministry; we attended their School of Ministry. It was here we were trained in prophetic ministry, and in many other areas of ministry. We got a lot of hands-on experience as well.

Joseph gained leadership experience in Potiphar's house and in jail. He was put over the affairs in the two places. Joseph's time in prison afforded him the opportunity to gain leadership skill, even though Joseph may not have known at the time that he was gaining experience in how to lead people.

Even though it was in prison, Joseph was well nurtured now for the role God had been preparing him for all along.

The famine affected the land of Canaan—it caused Joseph's brothers to come from Egypt to buy grain.

> *¹When Jacob saw that there was grain in Egypt, Jacob said to his sons, "Why do you look at one another?" ²And he said, "Indeed I have heard that there is grain in Egypt; go down to that place and buy for us there, that we may live and not die." ³So Joseph's ten brothers went down to buy grain in Egypt. ⁴But Jacob did not send Joseph's brother Benjamin with his brothers, for he said, "Lest some calamity befall him." ⁵And the sons of Israel went to buy grain among those who journeyed, for the famine was in the land of Canaan. ⁶Now Joseph was governor over the land; and it was he who sold to all the people of the land. And Joseph's brothers came and bowed down before him with their faces to the earth. ⁷Joseph saw his brothers and recognized them, but he acted as a stranger to them and spoke roughly to them. Then he said to them, "Where do you come from?" And they said, "From the land of Canaan to buy food. ⁸So Joseph recognized his brothers, but they did not recognize him. ⁹Then Joseph remembered the dreams which he had dreamed about them, and said to them, "You are spies! You have come to see the nakedness of the land! (Genesis 42:1-9)*

Joseph saw his brothers for the first time, but the remembrance of how he was sold into slavery by them must have aroused something in him. He spoke roughly to his brothers, but did not reveal his identity. He probably accused them falsely to see their reaction. If Joseph was out for revenge, he would have revealed his identity immediately to let them know the dream had come to pass. He would have told his guards to arrest them and would have planned a course of punishment for them.

It appears Joseph through the years came to a place of understanding. He apparently felt there was no need to exact revenge because what his brothers meant for evil, God used for His good.

Given that Joseph was second in command, Potiphar, who put him in jail before, was now subject to him. God had raised him above all the people who worked against him to destroy him.

> [8] *He raises the poor from the dust*
> *And lifts the beggar from the ash heap,*
> *To set them among princes*
> *And make them inherit the throne of glory.*
> *For the pillars of the earth are the LORD's,*
> *And He has set the world upon them. (1 Samuel 2:8)*

When you get to the nurturing stage, you are no longer interested in revenge, but instead you are more interested in doing the will of God. You care more about how the situation you face can glorify God. God vindicated Joseph; He raised him from the dunghill, and Joseph recognized that. Joseph matured.

I remember the word the lady at the clothing store gave me—that I would remember the pain only if I chose to think back on it; otherwise, God would bless us spiritually and physically so that we would not remember. This is exactly what happened to us. We forgot the pain of the past but held on to the lessons that we learned. In thinking about the situation, it became a blessing rather than a curse because, if it had not happened, I would not have found myself in the place I did. I had the opportunity to learn and grow.

EXERCISE

1. Share how God moved you from the challenging situation:___
   _____
   _____
   _____
   _____

2. What is different now?_____
   _____
   _____
   _____
   _____

3. What lessons have you learned?_____
   _____
   _____
   _____

4. Share how something you earned in the nurturing stage has helped to bring a solution to the challenging time of someone else. _____
   _____
   _____
   _____
   _____

5. Compare where you are now to where you were. Do you see any growth?_____
_____
_____
_____
_____

Thank the Lord, knowing He is going to use you to nurture other people because of the experience you have gained. Trust Him to create an opportunity for you daily, to pour into the life of someone.

MORE NOTES FROM GROUP SHARING

Chapter 7
YIELDEDNESS: The 'YES, Lord' Stage

total surrender, giving up control of your life to a superior authority

At this stage, you surrender to the will of God. It is no more what you want, but what He wants for you. You are ready to walk in the divine purpose of God for your life.

You now have an understanding of why you went through the different stages.

Joseph had a series of tests for his brothers, which you can read in Genesis, chapters 43 and 44. I am picking up from chapter 45, where Joseph revealed his identity to the brothers. He was not angry but instead reassured them; it was God who sent him to Egypt, not them.

> *¹Then Joseph could not restrain himself before all those who stood by him, and he cried out, "Make everyone go out from me!" So no one stood with him while Joseph made himself known to his brothers. ²And he wept aloud, and the Egyptians and the house of Pharaoh heard it. ³Then Joseph said to his brothers, "I am Joseph; does my father still live?" But his brothers could not answer him, for they were dismayed in his presence. ⁴And Joseph said to his brothers, "Please come near to me." So they came near. Then he said: "I am Joseph your brother, whom you sold into Egypt. ⁵"But now, do not therefore be grieved or angry with*

yourselves because you sold me here; for God sent me before you to preserve life. ⁶"For these two years the famine has been in the land, and there are still five years in which there will be neither plowing nor harvesting. ⁷"And God sent me before you to preserve a posterity for you in the earth, and to save your lives by a great deliverance. ⁸"So now it was not you who sent me here, but God; and He has made me a father to Pharaoh, and lord of all his house, and a ruler throughout all the land of Egypt." (Genesis 45:1-8)

Joseph, in the setback and testing stage, could not have confessed what he now confessed; God brought him to preserve a generation. This is maturity. You also can look back at your situation and be thankful that God took you through His refining fire. You are now able to say God did all He did to get you to this point. Whatever the point is, for each person the experience will be different.

In the new ministry, we found ourselves; we became elders; we had the opportunity to go on a mission trip to our homeland after being away for nine and a half years. We continued to thrive in the ministry. It was in this ministry that the Lord called us to start the ministry He had placed on our hearts five years prior. On October 1, 1999, we started the ministry called Chosen Remnant Christian Ministries, and God has been faithful to date.

Having received healing from my own broken heart, my husband and I were ready to serve the Body of Christ. We could relate to those that were hurting. Many people have passed through the ministry. We have seen God deliver and bring clarity to His calling on people's lives.

I will share one example of the many things that the Lord has done so far:

A friend invited me to her place to minister to two of her friends, but twenty-two people showed up. During ministry time, there was a guy there who I knew had no idea of what his purpose was, but God gave me prophetic utterance explaining how he was called to become a minister of the gospel.

The Lord talked through him about the weird experiences he had as a young child. This guy took the word spoken and ran with it. He attended Bible College. It was while at the Bible College that the Lord called him to become the youth pastor in their church. had over three hundred youth, and today he has a thriving church.

If God had not moved us, I would not have been able to get a strong foundation and training in the prophetic. It is in walking in the calling of God that He was able to use me to touch the life of this person.

In my closing remarks, I will share a few more things and some testimonies to encourage you. Unless we allow God to take charge of our lives, we may not walk in the fullness of His purpose. Jesus Christ came that we may have life and life more abundantly. It is in God you can experience that abundant life. Joseph as the Governor of Egypt had authority to do and undo. The dreams of Pharaoh came true: There were seven years of plenty and seven years of famine.

In Canaan, the children of Israel ran out of food, and Jacob sent some of his sons to go to Egypt to buy food. They did not recognize Joseph; they bowed to him (fulfillment of the first dream—Genesis 37:5-8). The next time they came and bowed to him again (fulfillment of the second dream—Genesis 37:9).

Eventually, the whole family moved to Egypt to live there (fulfillment of the dream God gave Abraham in which his descendants will be strangers in a foreign land—Genesis 15:13).

God sees the big picture, while we see a little at a time. The things you go through may be painful at first, but when you finally get to understand what God is doing, it becomes a thing of joy.

Sometimes we may be the forerunner, and, as a forerunner, you walk the path first to clear the thorns and thistles on the way for those who follow. In the clearing, you may sustain some injury, but God will soothe that for you. He smiles at you because you are fulfilling His plan.

When God gave Joseph the dream, He did not tell Joseph how he would arrive at his destination. Joseph did not know the journey would be interesting and challenging.

Jesus came as the forerunner that opened the way for us to cultivate a relationship with God. He died, and it is in the shedding of His blood that we have forgiveness of sin. Not only did He die: He rose again, and lives forevermore, and because of Him we will also live eternally.

One thing anyone walking towards their destiny would agree with is, at different stages, He continues to enlarge us. There may be new trials and testing but God intervenes; we learn what we need to learn, mature in it and move on.

I call them "T.I.N.Y" challenges compared to where God is taking you. Remember you will face another **Testing,** but you have the assurance; God will **intervene** at the right time. The Nurturing time brings you into a new experience, and you have the opportunity to say "**Y**es, Lord" again. It is another opportunity to die to anything that will become an obstacle to you on the Road to Destiny.

Every time you face a challenge, tell yourself, it is "T.I.N.Y." compared to what God is doing in your life. Until you reach the fullness of the purpose of God for your life, you will have obstacles to overcome. We are all not going to be at the same point at the same time, but sharing the different experiences becomes a source of encouragement.

The Lord moved us to another ministry; where we were was more of a training center. They eventually moved back to their country to start something there.

At this new ministry, things were fine, and we continued to enjoy God. I worked in the office, and my boss moved on and another came. The people in the office respected me, and we all had a great relationship with our former boss.

Another boss came who insisted we wear all black to work every day. Some people who came in have asked if we had a funeral going on at the church, so we suggested to our boss that she let us at least wear a different color of blouse under our suit. She told me the Lord gave her a scripture on which she was basing our wearing black upon. I told her I did not think it is what the scripture is saying. She became offended, called a meeting, told the others I was not in unity with them. She said they were free to wear something different under their outfits since I was not in agreement..

We continued with life until one day she and the senior pastor called me into a meeting. I was told to become her number-one cheerleader, act like she does because people respect me, and, if they see me do that, they will respect her, too. I told them I could be a cheerleader for her, but I am not framed that way, and it would be impossible for me to lose my own identity. I promised to always be there for her, but I could not take on a personality who is not me. People who know me will know it is not me at all.

The meeting continued. The senior pastor prophesied to me first. He said, "The Lord said even though you are gifted, your gift is way below her gift, and you were brought here to learn from her." He went further to say, "The Lord said you are a living stone, but a smaller stone in comparison to her as a living stone."

She also prophesied something but at this point, I could no longer hear anything, I just said to myself, "I reject it in Jesus's name." It took the grace of God and respect for my pastor as my spiritual head not to say anything. I thanked them and left.

All the way home, I felt like I was dreaming. I was hurt but kept my composure. I decided I was going to pray before responding to the word of prophecy. I was shocked; they will compare gifts when I have never walked or talked in a way to show any arrogance. I only minister in church as the opportunity arose.

After sleeping over it for two days, I wrote to my pastor to ask if I have in any way shown pride, as far as the prophetic gift is concerned. I also said there was nothing for me to boast about, because anything I have was given to me from above.

I said the Bible tells me that, if I compare my gift to another, I am not wise, so I would appreciate it if I can be shown where I have done that. I said thirdly, I do not believe the Father belittles on of his children for the other. It just did not sound like the Father I know.

I closed by saying, if I have offended in any way that brought that about, I apologize. Two days later, the senior pastor emailed a short note: "You are a beautiful daughter of the King."

Anyone would have expected us to leave the ministry, but we did not. The Lord eventually moved me into a new role, and we stayed with the ministry until He called us out to do something different. I was hurt, but I got over it and continued as if nothing happened. I was more interested in seeing the purpose of God come to fruition in the lives of His Children, and I focused more on that.

The experience showed me the nurturing of the past had truly matured me; otherwise, we would have tried to leave. Furthermore, I have come to understand you cannot leave a place unless the Lord releases you, or you may abort what he is doing. Below is the testimony of a lady I ministered to years after the incident. If I had walked away out of anger, how could God have used me to bless her?

TESTIMONY 1

Hi Margaret,

I wanted to thank you for being such a blessing to my family and especially Y. I know that she truly values and appreciates the time that you spend discussing the Gospel of John every Saturday.

On another note, I'm not sure if you remember who I am, but about 3 years ago you prophesied over my life that God would restore all things that I thought were lost in my life. You prophesied this during a time when I had experienced so much loss as a result of the poor choices that I had made in my life prior to rededicating my life to Christ about 6 months prior to the prophetic word. Within a year of that prophesy, all of the words that you spoke started to come to pass. Today I can say that the Lord's word has been fulfilled. Not only has he restored all that was lost, but he has given me more than what was lost; that you also prophesied.

Thank you for being such a strong woman of God. I truly admire you and I am grateful for everything that you are pouring into Y's life as well. I pray many blessings over you and your household.

To God Be the Glory,
Darra E

EXERCISE

1. You are now at the point where it is about Christ. Have you totally surrendered to His Lordship?_____
   _____
   _____
   _____
   _____

2. If the Lord requires you to do something that is out of your comfort zone, what will you say?_____
   _____
   _____
   _____
   _____

3. Share a situation in which you had to use the experience you gained to bless another._____
   _____
   _____
   _____
   _____

4. Share your thoughts on what you have gained from doing the study._____
   _____
   _____
   _____
   _____

MORE NOTES FROM SHARING

Chapter 8
CONCLUSION

The Lord told the children of Israel to spy out the land. He already informed them it was a land flowing with milk and honey, but He did not tell them about the giants in the land. Those giants became their challenge. Ten of the twelve spies saw a setback, but Joshua and Caleb saw a step forward. They understood God had given them the land and, no matter how things look, they were going to possess the land. Spying out the land took them a step closer to the fulfillment of the promise. It had nothing to do with them personally, but everything to do with their God who made them the promise.

What challenge is standing in your path as a giant at the moment? You look at where you are and who you are, and you do not see how you can overcome. You really have nothing to worry about, because Joshua and Caleb saw the giants too, but they believed the word of the Lord concerning the possession of the land. The statement they made is "we are able to possess the land." They were not looking at the ability of Joshua or Caleb. However, they were going in the Might of the Lord. In your circumstance, are you looking at your ability or at God, who can fight for you?

Be encouraged by this Psalm. It is a psalm sung by the pilgrims on their way to Jerusalem to worship God. It is a song that tells us there is no other person that can help but God. It is God who keeps His people. He is the one who keeps you too.

> *[1]I will lift up my eyes to the hills -- From whence comes my help? [2]My help comes from the LORD, Who made heaven and earth. [3]He will not allow your foot to be moved; He who keeps you will not slumber. [4]Behold, He who keeps Israel Shall neither slumber nor sleep. [5]The LORD is your keeper; The LORD is your shade at your right hand. [6]The sun shall not strike you by day, Nor the moon by night. [7]The LORD shall preserve you from all evil; He shall preserve your soul. [8]The LORD shall preserve your going out and your coming in From this time forth, and even forevermore. (Psalm 121:1-8)*

Christ is the Master Builder (I Cor. 3:10), and He is building you into the vessel he wants you to become.

Some people get a prophetic word or a dream from the Lord; they believe it will automatically happen. It does not work that way; first, it is conditional because you have to be obedient to follow the leading and direction of Holy Spirit. Secondly, you will meet giants (obstacles, challenges) on the way. But the good news is this: The Lord will never leave you nor forsake you.

Someone may challenge me, if they do not have a relationship with Jesus, by saying, "I am walking in my destiny because I am successful, and I can afford anything money can buy." To such a person, my question is, "Can money fill the emptiness you feel even though you are rich?" God is not against your being rich; it is He that gives the power to make wealth, but if God is not in it, **it is not good success**. Until we let go and let God, we will miss certain steps on The Road to Destiny.

When you yield to the Lordship of Christ, you now say "Lord, you have made me rich, but how do you want me to use the wealth you have given me?" What you do for the Kingdom of God is what will last. You may say "I already help people and I am a good person."

The Bible says our righteousness is as filthy rags before God (Isaiah 64:6). You must be robed in the Righteousness of God in Christ (II Corinthians 5:21). You do not need money to purchase salvation; you only need to confess your sins, turn away from them, believe in your heart that God raised Christ from the dead, and confess Him with your mouth, and you will be saved (Romans 10: 9).

You can accept Jesus Christ right now, and you will no longer have to walk the path of life alone. He will guide and direct you by His Spirit. He has a plan and purpose for your life greater than what you see now, so why not accept him and make him the Lord of your life. If you choose to, say this prayer:

Lord Jesus, I thank you for dying for me; I ask you to forgive my sins; I promise to turn away from them, never to return to them. I believe in my heart God raised you from the dead. I confess you with my mouth as the Lord and Savior of my life and according to your word. Now I receive the gift of salvation.

CONGRATULATIONS, you have just taken the first step in the right direction on your Road to Destiny. Share what you did with somebody or write to us at:

Chosen Remnant Christian Ministries
P. O. Box 800,
Powder Springs, GA 30127
chosenremnant@gmail.com
www.chosenremnant.org

If you find that rather than progressing you have slacked, get up, and start moving once again towards your destiny. I pray in Jesus name that the Lord will allow you to gain back the grounds you lost. AMEN!

What will you do differently?
_____
_____
_____
_____
_____
_____

LEARNING FROM MY MISTAKES

Everything that happened to me actually helped me to grow in the things of God. I learned from my mistakes, one being if the place fellowship does not believe in certain things, you can pray for them but you cannot force it on them. It will become rebellion if you are not careful. If you feel you are hindered from growing, maybe it is time to ask the Lord to lead you to where you need to be.

We must never rebel against authority. The Lord detests rebellion. Saul was instructed to utterly destroy the Amalekites until they are consumed but he did not do that; he took some of the things, claiming he was going to use them to make sacrifice to the Lord. God rejected him because of his disobedience.

> *[23] For rebellion is as the sin of witchcraft,*
> *And stubbornness is as iniquity and idolatry.*
> *Because you have rejected the word of the LORD,*
> *He also has rejected you from being king. (1 Samuel 15:23)*

The prophetic ministry faces a lot of resistance; I know and understand that now. I let the Lord lead me in the best way possible to deal with each situation I encounter. Some people are more open to the ministry, and some are not. Sometimes it is all because of bad experience; however, we cannot throw the baby out with the bath water.

We must learn to embrace the prophetic again. The Church cannot survive for too long without a new word from the Lord. Prophecy is the testimony of Jesus Christ. Without it, we just end up with a lot of good programs and have a form of godliness with no power.

The church will also lose a sense of what God is doing now and He wants to do in His Church, if we do not take the time to hear what He is saying to His Church. More of this will be discussed in my book <u>The Headless Church</u>.

Some of you reading may still be hurting from the past. The Lord is the Healer of the broken heart. You have to decide to shift your focus from what man has done to you to what God will do in you, for you, and through you. Learn from what happens.

One of the things I learned also is what not to do to other people. Let your confidence be in God and not in man. Appreciate the gift of God in His Church as well as appreciate your own God-given gift.

A few testimonies are listed below. These are as a result of allowing God to mold me into the vessel that is good for His use. He has blessed me with the opportunity to teach churches in the prophetic. These testimonies are to encourage you not to lose faith. Look unto Jesus, who is the author and the finisher of His purpose for you, and not at what man has done to you.

The pain we encounter pales in comparison to the lives He changes through us. Jesus saw you, He saw me, and He saw a dying world doomed for hell. He chose to lay down His life for us. The joy of our knowing the Father, and spending eternity with them drove Jesus to the cross.

If it were easy, Jesus would not have asked the Father to take the cup away—if it were possible—but because he was a yielded vessel, He said not his will but the will of the Father be done.

Because you have chosen to be a vessel of honor in His hands, all you can say now is, "God let your will be done in my life." Let go of the pain and look forward to doing great exploits for Him. Allow Him to use you for His glory.

He has called us to start a Church. It is another chapter on our Road to Destiny, but we know He is with us. The name of the Church is Harvestland International Christian Center. We believe many souls will be won into the Kingdom, and many hurting souls will be healed and restored in Jesus name. Thank you for reading.

God bless you.

TESTIMONIES

TESTIMONY 2

My names are Andrew Wanyonyi Wabwile, from Kitale town; in Kenya, East Africa. I am born again; Jesus is Lord and King of my life. I am married to Grace Wanyonyi, and we are blessed with six children.

God is always faithful no matter what happens in life, maybe frustration that comes from Satan. It may be sickness, lack or pains that come your way in life. This is what we call storm of life, and before you reach your destiny, you must come across it for your growth.

This is my testimony. I met Margaret, Anthony and Vickie from America in one of their training sessions. When Margaret was teaching in my city in the year 2007, I had made a decision of quitting the ministry to look for employment in Nairobi.

Through prophesy and the teaching, God spoke to me clearly that I should not leave the ministry. She said "do not leave the work of the Lord and go for employment, He knows what you are passing through, stand firm, wait He will make a way where there is no way."

I was disturbed by this prophecy it made my mind stagger. After teaching, she asked if there was anybody that would like to have prayers about the message. I was the first to go in front, she prayed for me.

At this time, I was pastoring a church in rural areas, in a village where the church could not support me because its members were from poor families, poorer than my family. I could not finish my education due to lack of funds because my father was poor too.

After the prophecy of the servant of God, Margaret, I decided to wait on the Lord. After Margaret left we continued communicating through Facebook and email. I have seen the hand of God considering the fact I use to work as a night guard.

The prophetic words have come to pass. I have visited Uganda, more than 20 times to preach the gospel. I have visited the following places twice, Rwanda, Burundi, Congo and Sudan, to preach. I have been to Tanzania four times just o preach the gospel.

My wife, Grace and I began project in June last year with 12 orphans in our home. God touched a missionary from Belgium brother Alex who works with Jesus Crew street Ministries, when he visited Kenya in 2010. I was his interpreter, he bought a small place my family and through him we receive support of food.

People now come into our home for Bible teaching. Members of Chosen Remnant and friends who have been supporting the servant of God in taking out the gospel, be blessed, you are sowing on fertile land. Keep on doing this good work, though you cannot do what she is doing, your prayers and financial support is very important

Thank Margaret, Rom 10:17 says, faith comes by hearing and hearing by the word of Christ. If you are reading this message, I encourage you to read Psalm 1:1-6.

God bless you Margaret, your ministry and your family. I now work with Jesus Crew Street Ministries; we preach about holiness Hebrews 12:14. We expect the Jesus Crew Team in June, 2014

Andrew Wanyonyi and Grace, Kitale, Kenya

TESTIMONY 3

I met Pastor Margaret in 2011 at my church's prophetic conference in Lagos, Nigeria. The ministration was awesome, and she gave us her Facebook ID that we could hook up with her there which I did. I also joined Chosen Remnant Prophetic Forum on Facebook. I can say I became an active commentator on the page. I never knew Pastor Margaret was observing me.

In 2012, precisely Jan 12th, I lost my dad due to an illness that we could not take him to the hospital then due to the nationwide protest in Nigeria, as a result of total subsidy removal by the Federal govt. On July 2nd 2012, my mom passed on as a result of thinking so much about my dad's demise. Due to the incidence, I did not comment on the forum for a while.

Pastor Margaret checked to see what the reason was for the prolonged silence on the page. I told her, and she called my line. She checked on what I was doing at the time as well as how my siblings were doing. I told her I was in school, and how siblings were faring. She continued to check on me from time to time.

In October, I had a need for a laptop in school, through their ministry, sent me the money. In 2013, she was in Nigeria. I saw her again; she prayed with me and also encouraged me. She asked me to let her know when my next school fees will be due, she promised the ministry will support me with it, so I do not have to scramble about for it.

In October, she sent me the fees for my school fees. In January 2014, she also introduced me to a sister of hers, whom she said she has spoken to about me. January 17th 2014, her sister visited me in my house with her husband, and they brought loads of food items for me and my youngest brother, also on the 2nd of March 2014, she also came with food items and gave us money. She always reminds me that God is the father to the fatherless.

In March 2014, Pastor Margaret sent me money to cover our annual yearly rent for the place I stay with my brother. With me not having to worry about rent, I can see the faithfulness of God in my life. I also have been made to trust in God the more. I believe in the word I heard the night my mother passed on, that it is well.

I have been encouraged by those words, every time God shows up miraculously for me. My meeting with Pastor Margaret was ordained by God Himself to fulfill destiny. I now boldly tell people that I don't have to worry about food or clothing for me. I know God has taken that up by Himself, and will take care of other things for me as well.

May God bless Pastors Anthony & Margaret Sowemimo richly. I have a more to write, but time will not permit me. I hope to have the opportunity to share this story some in the future.

Our steps are truly ordered by God, from social media friendship to a real-life developing friendship.

Ogungbure, Samuel Seun.

+2348050658457, forensictutor@gmail.com

Made in the USA
Columbia, SC
28 February 2025